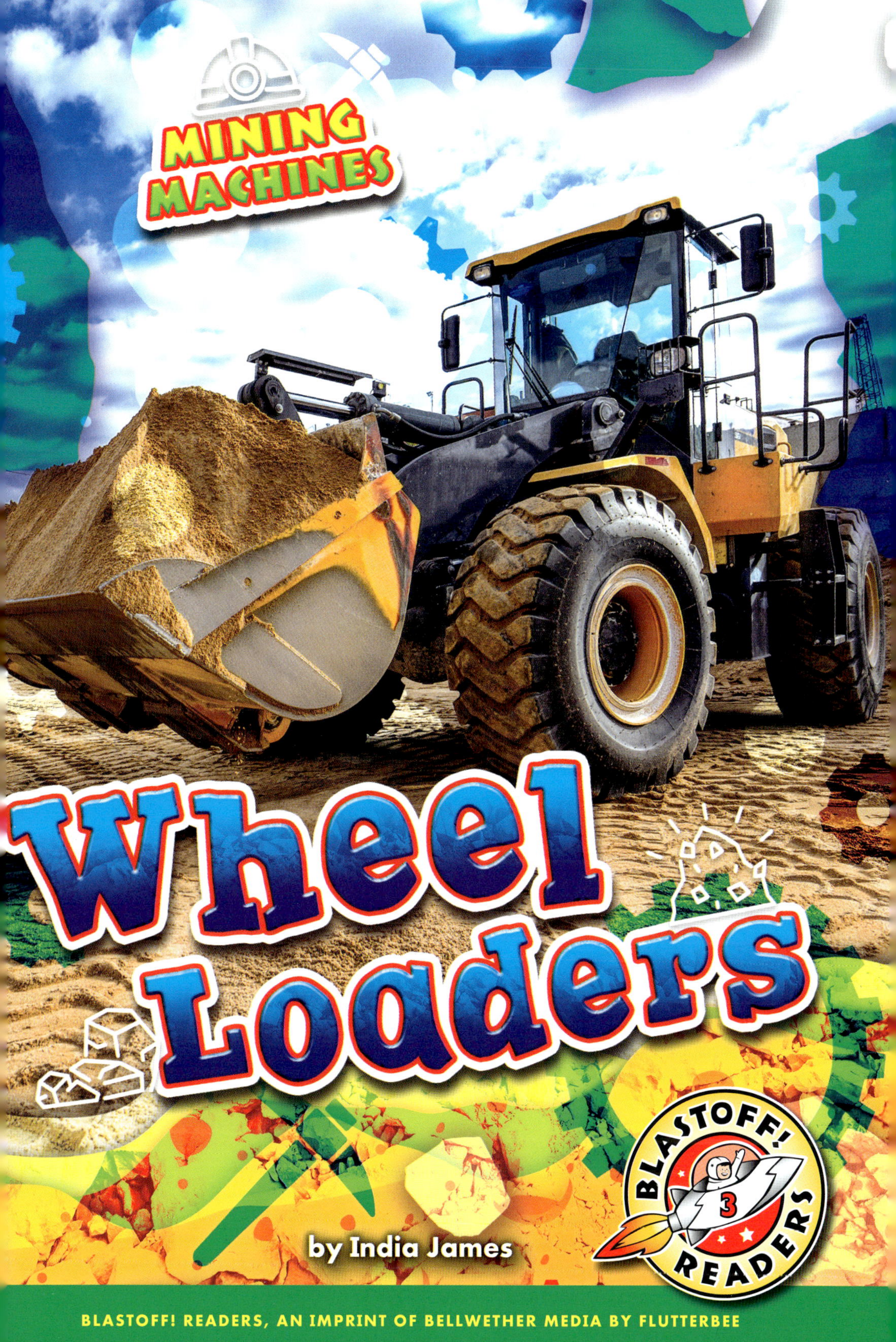

BLASTOFF! READERS, AN IMPRINT OF BELLWETHER MEDIA BY FLUTTERBEE

Blastoff! Readers are carefully developed by literacy experts to build reading stamina and move students toward fluency by combining standards-based content with developmentally appropriate text.

Level 1 provides the most support through repetition of high-frequency words, light text, predictable sentence patterns, and strong visual support.

Level 2 offers early readers a bit more challenge through varied sentences, increased text load, and text-supportive special features.

Level 3 advances early-fluent readers toward fluency through increased text load, less reliance on photos, advancing concepts, longer sentences, and more complex special features.

★ **Blastoff! Universe**

Reading Level

Grade K

Grades 1–3

Grade 4

This edition first published in 2027 by Bellwether Media, Inc.

Library of Congress Cataloging-in-Publication Data is available at www.loc.gov or upon request from the publisher.

ISBN: 9798898800741 (hardcover)
ISBN: 9798898801984 (ebook)

Editor: Kieran Downs Designer: Jeffrey Kollock

Printed in the United States of America, North Mankato, MN.

Table of Contents

What Are Wheel Loaders?

Wheel loaders are important machines. They are used for many mining jobs.

Wheel loaders often have a bucket. The bucket can carry a lot of dirt and **ore**.

Wheel loaders can move heavy **loads**. They can also lift **waste**.

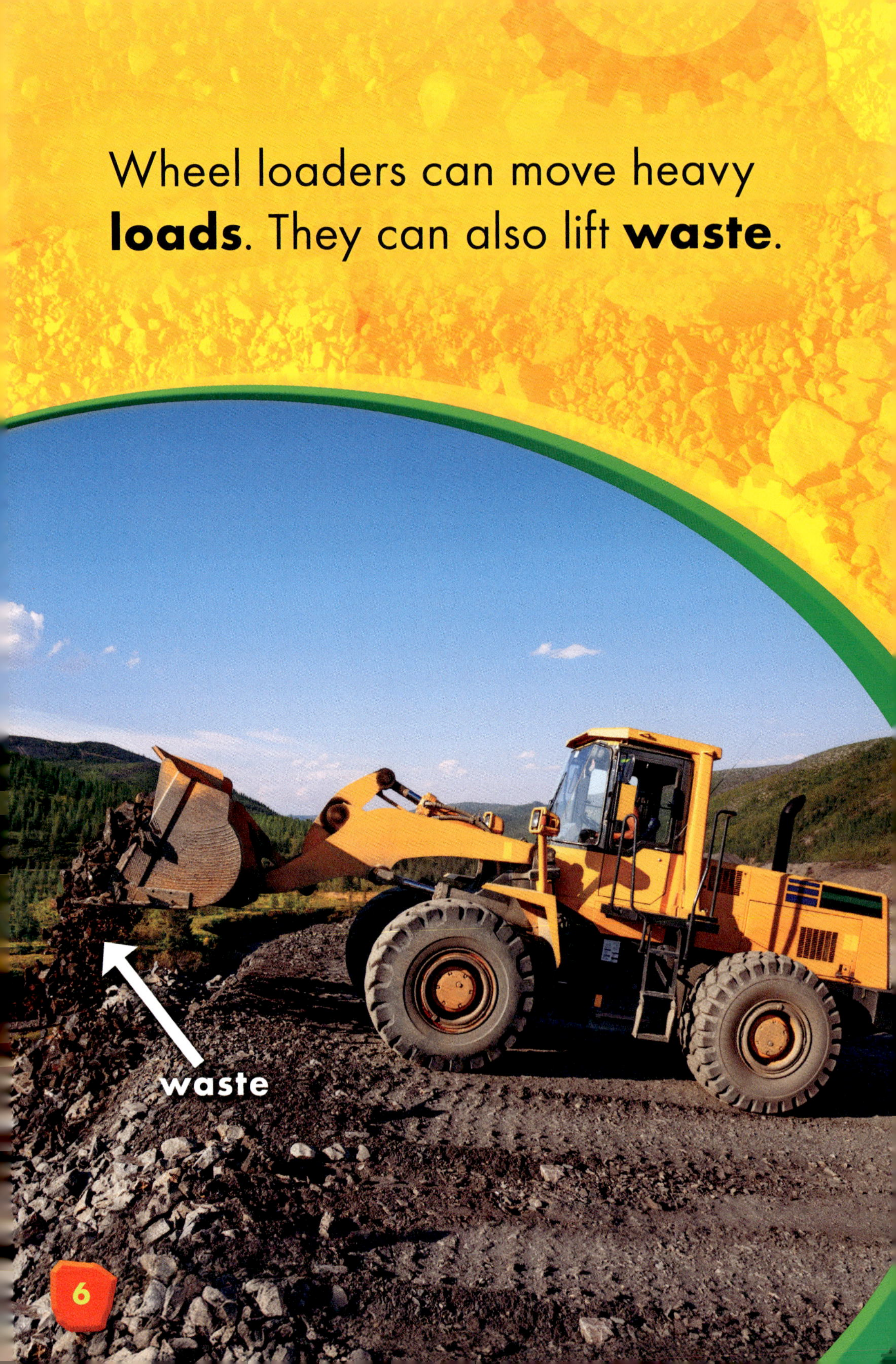

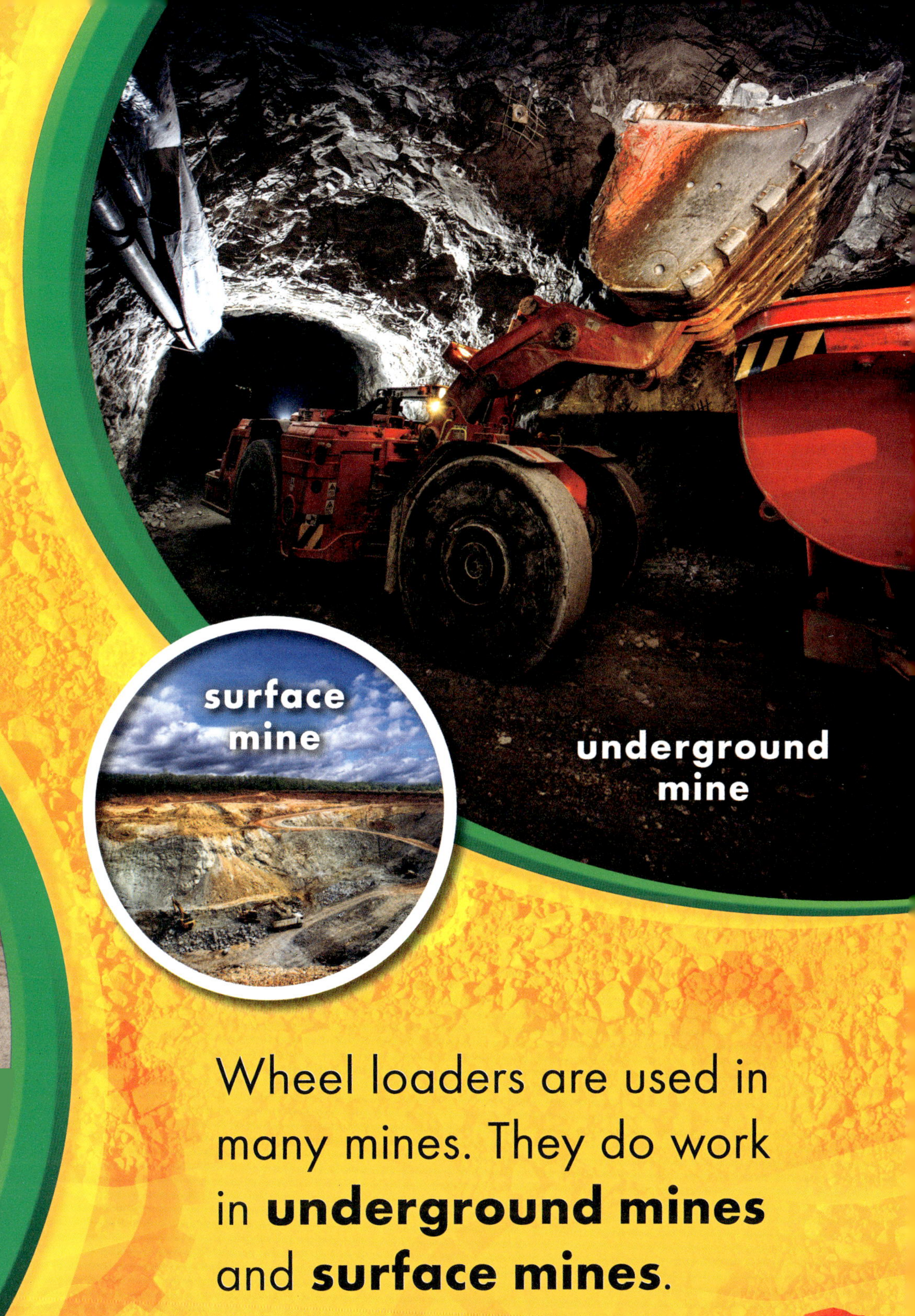

Wheel loaders are used in many mines. They do work in **underground mines** and **surface mines**.

There are many different types of wheel loaders. **Compact** wheel loaders are the smallest.

Wheel loaders also come in medium and large sizes. Larger loaders can move more dirt in one scoop.

Parts of a Wheel Loader

Wheel loaders have four big wheels. Wheels make it easy for the machine to move.

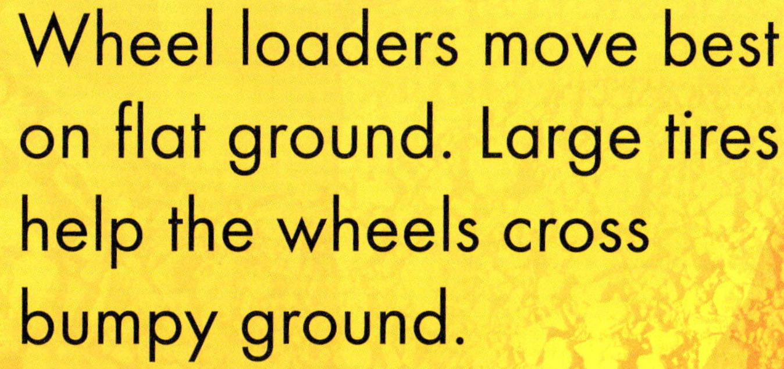

Wheel loaders move best on flat ground. Large tires help the wheels cross bumpy ground.

Wheel loaders have two long **booms**. They connect to the main machine on one end.

The other end connects to the bucket. The booms raise and lower it into place.

Wheel loaders use their buckets to scoop and lift dirt and **materials**.

The buckets can be taken off. They can be replaced with tools for digging or grabbing.

Wheel Loaders at Work

Wheel loaders work with other machines. They lift things that other machines dig up.

Wheel loaders can move loads to where they are needed. They can also lift material into dump trucks.

dump truck

A driver can run a wheel loader without anyone else. All of the controls are in the **cab**.

Sometimes a **spotter** helps the driver. The spotter can watch for **obstacles** on the ground.

Wheel loaders can be big or small. Big wheel loaders are useful in mines to lift very heavy loads.

Wheel Loader Profile

Komatsu WA900

weighs 256,618 pounds (116,400 kilograms)

bucket holds 19 cubic yards (14.5 cubic meters) of material

moves with 899 horsepower

Wheels, buckets, and other tools make the wheel loader a powerful mining machine!

Glossary

booms—long arms on a wheel loader

cab—the part of a wheel loader where the driver sits

compact—small or close together

loads—things being carried

materials—things that are used to help make something else

obstacles—objects that stand in the way

ore—a valuable material that occurs naturally in the earth

spotter—a person who watches for people or things that could be dangerous

surface mines—mines that get materials from near Earth's surface

underground mines—mines that get materials from under Earth's surface

waste—material that is not needed

To Learn More

AT THE LIBRARY

James, India. *Mining Shovels*. Minneapolis, Minn.: Bellwether Media, 2027.

James, Ryan. *Excavators*. New York, N.Y.: Crabtree Publishing, 2025.

Rogers, Marie. *Huge Earthmovers*. New York, N.Y.: PowerKids Press, 2022.

ON THE WEB

FACTSURFER

Factsurfer.com gives you a safe, fun way to find more information.

1. Go to www.factsurfer.com.
2. Enter "wheel loaders" into the search box and click 🔍.
3. Select your book cover to see a list of related content.

Index

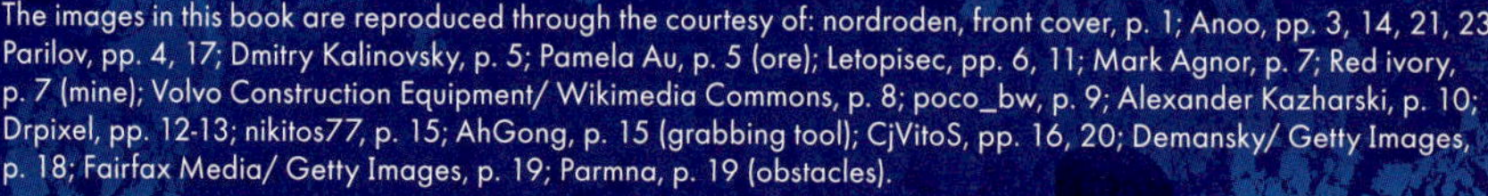

The images in this book are reproduced through the courtesy of: nordroden, front cover, p. 1; Anoo, pp. 3, 14, 21, 23; Parilov, pp. 4, 17; Dmitry Kalinovsky, p. 5; Pamela Au, p. 5 (ore); Letopisec, pp. 6, 11; Mark Agnor, p. 7; Red ivory, p. 7 (mine); Volvo Construction Equipment/ Wikimedia Commons, p. 8; poco_bw, p. 9; Alexander Kazharski, p. 10; Drpixel, pp. 12-13; nikitos77, p. 15; AhGong, p. 15 (grabbing tool); CjVitoS, pp. 16, 20; Demansky/ Getty Images, p. 18; Fairfax Media/ Getty Images, p. 19; Parmna, p. 19 (obstacles).